W9-DEH-781

PROBLEM SOLVING 4 Today

Daily
Skill Practice

Kindergarten

Carson-Dellosa Publishing LLC
Greensboro, North Carolina

Credits
Author: Jennifer B. Stith
Copy Editor: Angela Triplett

Visit *carsondellosa.com* for correlations to Common Core, state, national, and Canadian provincial standards.

Carson-Dellosa Publishing LLC
PO Box 35665
Greensboro, NC 27425 USA
carsondellosa.com

© 2019, Carson-Dellosa Publishing LLC. The purchase of this material entitles the buyer to reproduce worksheets and activities for classroom use only—not for commercial resale. Reproduction of these materials for an entire school or district is prohibited. No part of this book may be reproduced (except as noted above), stored in a retrieval system, or transmitted in any form or by any means (mechanically, electronically, recording, etc.) without the prior written consent of Carson-Dellosa Publishing LLC.

Printed in the USA • All rights reserved.

ISBN 978-1-4838-5014-6
01-312181151

Table of Contents

Introduction

Problem Solving 4 Today: Daily Skill Practice is a comprehensive yet quick and easy-to-use supplement to any classroom math curriculum. This series will strengthen students' problem-solving skills as they review and use strategies to solve word problems in numbers, operations, algebraic thinking, measurement, data, and geometry.

This book covers 40 weeks of daily problem-solving practice. Essential problem-solving skills are practiced each day during a four-day period with a problem-solving strategy introduced at the beginning of each week. Students are encouraged to solve the problems each day using the specified strategy. On the fifth day, an assessment is given to allow students to prove their competency in using the weekly strategy. Although the strategies are presented in a consecutive format, they can be used in any order.

Various problem-solving skills and strategies are reinforced throughout the book through activities that align to state standards. To view these standards, see the Standards Alignment Chart on page 7.

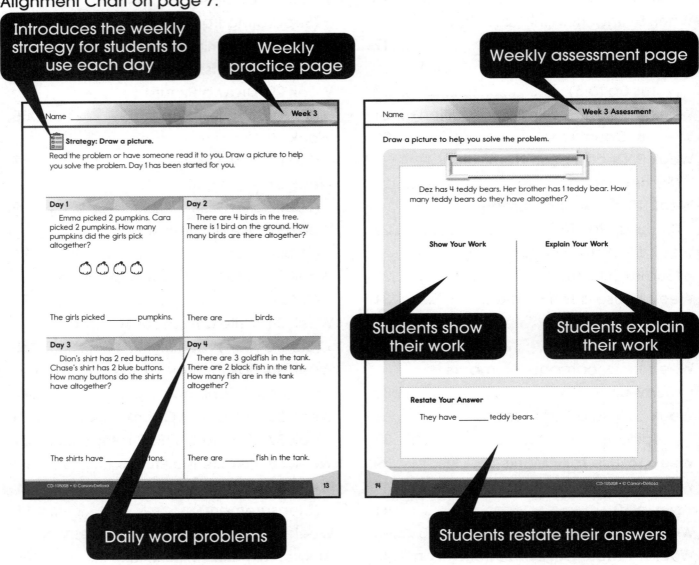

CD-105008 • © Carson-Dellosa

Solving word problems is an essential skill that every student must master. Developing and practicing problem-solving strategies enables students to deal more effectively and successfully with most types of mathematical problems.

With this series, a word problem will be presented each day for students to solve using a strategy that is intended to work well with the problem. Teachers should review and discuss the strategy and its applications at the beginning of each week. The word problems can then be given as part of a morning work routine, given as a nightly homework assignment, used in math journals, or cut apart and placed in a math center. The weekly assessment page is useful to have students show the steps they took to solve the word problem and to explain their reasoning.

The Problem-Solving Process

When solving math problems, students should be encouraged to follow this general problem-solving process as well as to develop and use their own problem-solving strategies.

Understand
- Restate the problem in your own words.
- What facts/information/data are given?
- What are you being asked to find?
- What information is missing or not needed?

Plan
- Which strategy should I use?
- Have I solved similar problems before?

Act
- Implement a strategy.
- Check each step of the plan as you work it.

Reflect
- Have you answered the question?
- Is the answer reasonable and accurate?
- Can you find another method or work backward to check your work?

Tracking Problem-Solving Skills

Have students use the reproducible on page 6 to keep track of their understanding of solving word problems. Four times during the year, have students complete the first column by adding the date and then drawing the appropriate symbol for each I Can . . . statement using the key under the chart. Repeat several times to show progress throughout the year. Have students answer the prompts at the bottom of the page to assess their overall learning.

Name _____

Word Problems

Skill	Date	Date	Date	Date
I can choose the correct operation.				
I can identify key words.				
I can use a drawing.				
I can use a number sentence.				
I can explain my answer.				
I can solve addition word problems.				
I can solve subtraction word problems.				
I can solve word problems involving measurement.				
I can solve word problems involving shapes.				

Ratings	✗ = not yet	? = maybe	✔ = yes

One thing I understand well is

One thing I can improve on is

CD-105008 • © Carson-Dellosa

Standards Alignment Chart

State Standards*		Week(s)
Counting and Cardinality		
Know number names and the count sequence.	K.CC.1–K.CC.3	1, 2, 8, 9, 18, 19, 26, 31
Count to tell the number of objects.	K.CC.4, K.CC.5	1, 2, 8, 9, 18, 19, 26, 31
Operations and Algebraic Thinking		
Understand addition as putting together and adding to, and understand subtraction as taking apart and taking from.	K.OA.1–K.OA.5	3–38
Measurement and Data		
Describe and compare measurable attributes.	K.MD.1, K.MD.2	39
Geometry		
Identify and describe shapes (squares, circles, triangles, rectangles, hexagons, cubes, cones, cylinders, and spheres).	K.G.1–K.G.3	40
Analyze, compare, create, and compose shapes.	K.G.4–K.G.6	40

* © Copyright 2010. National Governors Association Center for Best Practices and Council of Chief State School Officers. All rights reserved.

The research is clear that family involvement is strongly linked to student success. Support for student learning at home improves student achievement in school. Educators should not underestimate the significance of this connection.

The skill-building format of this book creates an opportunity to expand this school-to-home connection. Students are encouraged to practice their word problem-solving skills at home. Parents and guardians can use the reproducible strategy sheet (below) to help their students solve word problems at home during the week. The CUBES chart can also be used in the classroom by posting it in a math center or allowing students to glue it into their math journals.

In order to make the school-to-home connection successful for students and their families, it may be helpful to reach out to them with an introductory letter. Explain the problem-solving process and the CUBES strategy. Encourage them to offer suggestions or feedback along the way.

CUBES

Problem-Solving Strategy

C Circle the numbers.

U Underline the question.

B Box the key words.

E Eliminate extra information.

E Evaluate: What steps do I take?

S Solve and check.

© Carson-Dellosa

CD-105008 • © Carson-Dellosa

Strategy: Color the objects as you count.

Color and count the objects to find how many.

There are ___5___ butterflies.

Day 1	**Day 2**

There are _____ cars.

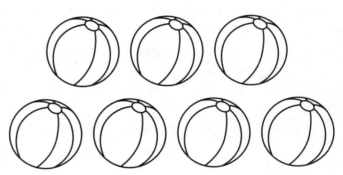

There are _____ balls.

Day 3	**Day 4**

There are _____ stars.

There are _____ cups.

Color and count the objects to find how many.

Show Your Work

Explain Your Work

Restate Your Answer

There are _____ flowers.

CD-105008 • © Carson-Dellosa

Strategy: Mark each object as you count.

Mark and count the objects to find how many.

There are ___6___ cats.

Day 1

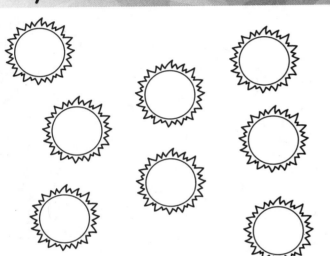

There are _____ suns.

Day 2

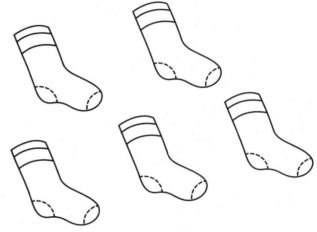

There are _____ socks.

Day 3

There are _____ leaves.

Day 4

There are _____ mugs.

Mark and count the objects to find how many.

Show Your Work

Explain Your Work

Restate Your Answer

There are _____ birds.

Strategy: Draw a picture.

Read the problem or have someone read it to you. Draw a picture to help you solve the problem. Day 1 has been started for you.

Day 1	**Day 2**

Day 1

Emma picked 2 pumpkins. Cara picked 2 pumpkins. How many pumpkins did the girls pick in all?

The girls picked _____ pumpkins in all.

Day 2

There are 4 birds in the tree. There is 1 bird on the ground. How many birds are there altogether?

There are _____ birds altogether.

Day 3

Dion's shirt has 2 red buttons. Chase's shirt has 2 blue buttons. How many buttons do the shirts have altogether?

The shirts have _____ buttons altogether.

Day 4

There are 3 goldfish in the tank. There are 2 black fish in the tank. How many fish are in the tank altogether?

There are _____ fish in the tank altogether.

Draw a picture to help you solve the problem.

Dez has 4 teddy bears. Her brother has 1 teddy bear. How many teddy bears do they have altogether?

Show Your Work	**Explain Your Work**

Restate Your Answer

They have _____ teddy bears altogether.

CD-105008 • © Carson-Dellosa

Strategy: Circle the numbers.

Read the problem or have someone read it to you. Circle the numbers you will use. Solve. Day 1 has been started for you.

Day 1	Day 2
Jay has ③ toy cars. His dad gives him ②more toy cars. How many cars does Jay have in all?	Ben has 4 rocks. His friend gives him 1 more rock. How many rocks does Ben have in all?
Jay has _____ cars in all.	Ben has _____ rocks in all.
Day 3	**Day 4**
Jess has 3 beads. Her sister gives her 1 more bead. How many beads does Jess have in all?	Sara has 2 dolls. Her mom gives her 2 more dolls. How many dolls does Sara have in all?
Jess has _____ beads in all.	Sara has _____ dolls in all.

Circle the numbers to help you solve the problem.

Luke has 2 apples. His grandma gives him 3 more apples. How many apples does Luke have in all?

Show Your Work

Explain Your Work

Restate Your Answer

Luke has _____ apples in all.

Strategy: Underline the question.

Read the problem or have someone read it to you. Underline the question to help you solve the problem. Day 1 has been started for you.

Day 1	Day 2
Amy has 3 bows. She makes 1 more bow. <u>How many bows does Amy have now?</u>	Brad rolled 2 dice. His sister rolled 2 dice. How many dice did they roll in all?
Amy has _____ bows now.	They rolled _____ dice in all.

Day 3	Day 4
Emily has 1 banana. Her mom buys 2 more bananas. How many bananas do they have now?	Kade blew up 4 balloons for the party. His brother blew up 1 balloon. How many balloons did they blow up in all?
They have _____ bananas now.	They blew up _____ balloons in all.

Underline the question to help you solve the problem.

Lisa saw 2 lions at the zoo. Erin saw 3 lions at the zoo. How many lions did they see in all?

Show Your Work	**Explain Your Work**

Restate Your Answer

They saw _____ lions in all.

Strategy: Box the key words.

Read the problem or have someone read it to you. Draw a box around the key words that tell you which operation to use. Day 1 has been started for you.

Day 1	Day 2
Carla made 3 tacos. Her mom made 1 taco. How many tacos did they make altogether?	Cory has 2 jars of candy. Dave has 1 jar of candy. How many jars of candy do they have in all?
They made _____ tacos altogether.	They have _____ jars in all.
Day 3	**Day 4**
Tatum gave her dog 2 treats. Her dad gave her dog 2 more treats. How many total treats did Tatum's dog get?	Vivian planted 3 seeds in one pot. She planted 2 seeds in another pot. How many seeds did Vivian plant in all?
Tatum's dog got _____ total treats.	Vivian planted _____ seeds in all.

Draw a box around the key words to help you solve the problem.

Bryce saw 4 buses on his way to school. He saw 1 bus on the way home. How many buses did Bryce see in all?

Show Your Work	**Explain Your Work**

Restate Your Answer

Bryce saw _____ buses in all.

CD-105008 • © Carson-Dellosa

Strategy: Use a five frame.

Read the problem or have someone read it to you. Draw dots in the frame to help you solve the problem. Day 1 has been started for you.

Day 1

Mario has 2 cats. Kevin has 1 cat. How many cats do the boys have in all?

The boys have _____ cats in all.

Day 2

Grandma made 1 pie on Sunday. She made 3 pies on Monday. How many pies did Grandma make in all?

Grandma made _____ pies in all.

Day 3

Ella put 2 cups on the table. Her mom put 2 cups on the table. How many cups did they put on the table in all?

They put _____ cups on the table in all.

Day 4

Wyatt picked 4 carrots from the garden. His mom picked 1 carrot. How many carrots did they pick in all?

They picked _____ carrots in all.

Draw dots in the frame to help you solve the problem.

Carter hit 2 baseballs over the fence. Dad hit 3 baseballs over the fence. How many baseballs did they hit over the fence in all?

Show Your Work

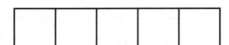

Explain Your Work

Restate Your Answer

They hit _____ baseballs over the fence in all.

CD-105008 • © Carson-Dellosa

Strategy: Count on.

Read the problem or have someone read it to you. Count on your fingers to help you solve the problem.

Day 1

Ava saw 3 turtles on the log. Bill saw 2 more turtles on the log. How many turtles did they see in all?

They saw _____ turtles in all.

Day 2

Lila put 2 stickers on her card. Elle put 2 stickers on her card. How many stickers did they use in all?

They used _____ stickers in all.

Day 3

Finn read 1 book in the morning. He read 2 books at night. How many books did Finn read in all?

Finn read _____ books in all.

Day 4

Chen took out 3 pencils from his bag. He took out 1 more pencil from his bag. How many pencils did Chen take out of his bag in all?

Chen took out _____ pencils from his bag in all.

Count on your fingers to help you solve the problem.

Tina put 3 berries in her bowl. She put 1 more berry in her bowl. How many berries did Tina put in her bowl in all?

Show Your Work	**Explain Your Work**

Restate Your Answer

Tina put _____ berries in her bowl in all.

CD-105008 • © Carson-Dellosa

Strategy: Decompose numbers.

Read the problem or have someone read it to you. Think about how a number can be made up of smaller parts. For example, 4 can be made up of 2 + 2 or 3 + 1. Color the picture to help you solve the problem.

Day 1

There are 4 bunnies in the grass. Some bunnies are brown. Some bunnies are white. How many bunnies could be brown? How many bunnies could be white?

_____ white bunnies
_____ brown bunnies

Day 2

Nicole made 3 sandwiches. Some were jelly sandwiches. Some were cheese sandwiches. How many could be jelly? How many could be cheese?

_____ jelly sandwiches
_____ cheese sandwiches

Day 3

Max has 5 crayons. Some crayons are red. Some crayons are blue. How many could be red? How many could be blue?

_____ red crayons
_____ blue crayons

Day 4

The teddy bear has 4 buttons. Some buttons are black. Some buttons are green. How many buttons could be black? How many buttons could be green?

_____ black buttons
_____ green buttons

Color the picture to help you solve the problem.

Daisy the dog is wearing 5 bows. Some are pink. Some are purple. How many bows could be pink? How many bows could be purple?

Show Your Work	**Explain Your Work**

Restate Your Answer

There could be _____ pink bows and_____ purple bows.

Strategy: Circle the numbers.

Read the problem or have someone read it to you. Circle the numbers you will use to help you solve the problem. Day 1 has been started for you.

Day 1

Grant has ④ toy trucks. His dad gives him ③ more toy trucks. How many trucks does Grant have in all?

Grant has _____ trucks in all.

Day 2

Bo has 4 superheroes. His friend gives him 5 more superheroes. How many superheroes does Bo have in all?

Bo has _____ superheroes in all.

Day 3

Maya made 6 bracelets for her friend. She made 2 bracelets for her sister. How many bracelets did Maya make in all?

Maya made _____ bracelets in all.

Day 4

Hana has 5 gel pens. Her mom gave her 3 more gel pens. How many gel pens does Hana have in all?

Hana has _____ gel pens in all.

Circle the numbers to help you solve the problem.

Leah picked 4 flowers for her mom. She picked 6 flowers for her grandma. How many flowers did Leah pick in all?

Show Your Work

Explain Your Work

Restate Your Answer

Leah picked _____ flowers in all.

CD-105008 • © Carson-Dellosa

Name _____

 Strategy: Draw a picture.

Read the problem or have someone read it to you. Draw a picture to help you solve the problem. Day 1 has been started for you.

Day 1	Day 2

Day 1

Warren has 5 toy planes. He gets 2 more planes from his dad. How many toy planes does Warren have now?

✈ ✈ ✈ ✈ ✈   ✈ ✈

Warren has _____ toy planes now.

Day 2

Reba read 3 books about dogs. She read 3 books about cats. How many books did Reba read altogether?

Reba read _____ books altogether.

Day 3

Colby gave his mom 4 flowers. He gave his sister 5 flowers. How many flowers did Colby give in all?

Colby gave _____ flowers in all.

Day 4

Brooke felt 2 raindrops. Then, she felt 6 more raindrops. How many raindrops did Brooke feel in all?

Brooke felt _____ raindrops in all.

Draw a picture to help you solve the problem.

Gavin sees 8 hippos playing in the mud. He sees 1 more hippo join them. How many hippos does Gavin see in all?

Show Your Work	**Explain Your Work**

Restate Your Answer

Gavin sees _____ hippos in all.

CD-105008 • © Carson-Dellosa

Strategy: Use a ten frame.

Read the problem or have someone read it to you. Draw dots in the frame to help you solve the problem. Day 1 has been started for you.

Day 1

Brian found 6 rocks. His brother found 2 rocks. How many rocks did they find in all?

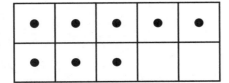

They found _____ rocks in all.

Day 2

There are 3 frogs on a log. Then, 4 more frogs hop onto the log. How many frogs are on the log now?

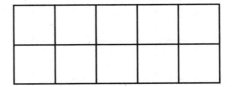

There are _____ frogs on the log.

Day 3

Anna has 9 markers. Her teacher gives her 1 more marker. How many markers does Anna have now?

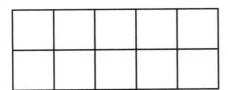

Anna has _____ markers now.

Day 4

George caught 4 fish. His brother caught 5 fish. How many fish did they catch altogether?

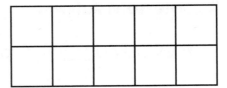

They caught _____ fish altogether.

Draw dots in the frame to help you solve the problem.

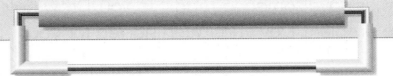

Dawn raked 5 piles of leaves. Her little sister raked 2 piles of leaves. How many piles of leaves did they rake in all?

Show Your Work	**Explain Your Work**
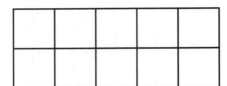	

Restate Your Answer

They raked _____ piles of leaves in all.

CD-105008 • © Carson-Dellosa

Strategy: Act it out.

Read the problem or have someone read it to you. Act out the problem with objects to help you solve the problem.

Day 1

Lisa drew 2 birds sitting on a branch in a tree. She drew 6 birds flying in the sky. How many birds did Lisa draw in all?

Lisa drew _____ birds in all.

Day 2

Nick counted 4 crackers on his plate. He counted 3 crackers on his friend's plate. How many crackers did Nick count in all?

Nick counted _____ crackers in all.

Day 3

Franny read 5 books this week. She read 2 books last week. How many books did Franny read altogether?

Franny read _____ books altogether.

Day 4

Chang took out 8 coins from his pocket. He took out 1 more coin from his pocket. How many coins did Chang take out of his pocket in all?

Chang took out _____ coins from his pocket in all.

Act out the problem with objects to help you solve the problem.

There are 6 clowns in the parade. Then, 3 more clowns join the parade. How many total clowns are in the parade?

Show Your Work

Explain Your Work

Restate Your Answer

There are _____ clowns in the parade.

CD-105008 • © Carson-Dellosa

Name _____

 Strategy: Decompose numbers.

Read the problem or have someone read it to you. Color the pictures to help you solve the problem.

Day 1	Day 2

Day 1

There are 9 butterflies on the bush. Some butterflies are orange. Some butterflies are yellow. How many butterflies could be orange? How many butterflies could be yellow?

_____ orange butterflies

_____ yellow butterflies

Day 2

Zane counted 6 clouds in the sky. Some were white. Some were gray. How many clouds could be white? How many clouds could be gray?

_____ white clouds

_____ gray clouds

Day 3

Mia lines up her 8 marbles. Some marbles are red. Some marbles are blue. How many could be red? How many could be blue?

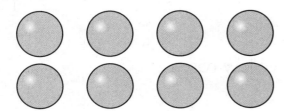

_____ red marbles

_____ blue marbles

Day 4

The farmer finds 9 eggs. Some eggs are white. Some eggs are brown. How many eggs could be white? How many eggs could be brown?

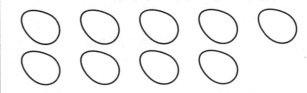

_____ white eggs

_____ brown eggs

Color the picture to help you solve the problem.

Jamie picks 7 roses. Some roses are pink. Some roses are yellow. How many roses could be pink? How many roses could be yellow?

Show Your Work	**Explain Your Work**

Restate Your Answer

_____ pink roses   _____ yellow roses

CD-105008 • © Carson-Dellosa

Strategy: Use a number line.

Read the problem or have someone read it to you. Use the number line to count on and solve the problem. Day 1 has been started for you.

Day 1	Day 2
Chloe sang 2 songs in the show. Her friend sang 4 songs in the show. How many songs did they sing in all?	Ben collects 5 gems. His aunt gives him 4 more gems. How many gems does Ben have in all?

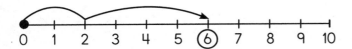

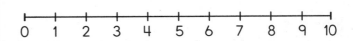

They sang _____ songs in all.

Ben has _____ gems in all.

Day 3	Day 4
The big dog ate 6 bones. The small dog ate 2 bones. How many bones did both dogs eat in all?	There are 3 bees on the flower. Then, 4 more bees join them. How many bees are on the flower now?

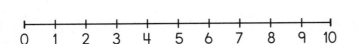

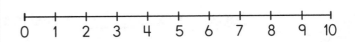

The dogs ate _____ bones in all.

There are _____ bees on the flower.

Use the number line to count on and solve the problem.

Jenna made 5 wishes before blowing out her birthday candles. Then, she made 1 more. How many wishes did Jenna make in all?

Show Your Work

| | | | | | | | | | | |
|0|1|2|3|4|5|6|7|8|9|10|

Explain Your Work

Restate Your Answer

Jenna made _____ wishes in all.

CD-105008 • © Carson-Dellosa

Strategy: Use tally marks.

Read the problem or have someone read it to you. Draw tally marks to help you solve the problem. Day 1 has been started for you.

Day 1	Day 2
The bike shop sold 5 bikes on Monday. They sold 2 bikes on Tuesday. How many bikes did they sell in all? The bike shop sold _____ bikes in all.	There are 7 penguins on the ice. There are 3 penguins in the water. How many penguins are there in all? There are _____ penguins in all.

Day 3	Day 4
John counted 2 photos on the wall. He counted 6 photos on the table. How many photos did John count in all? John counted _____ photos in all.	Mrs. Lee counted 6 runners finishing the race. She counted 3 more runners still in the race. How many runners were there in all? There were _____ runners in all.

Draw tally marks to help you solve the problem.

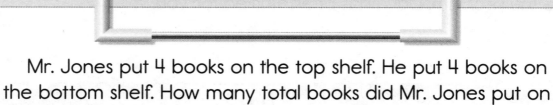

Mr. Jones put 4 books on the top shelf. He put 4 books on the bottom shelf. How many total books did Mr. Jones put on the shelf?

Show Your Work	Explain Your Work

Restate Your Answer

Mr. Jones put _____ books on the shelf.

CD-105008 • © Carson-Dellosa

Strategy: Use a ten frame to make 10.

Read the problem or have someone read it to you. Draw dots in the frame to make 10 and help you solve the problem. Day 1 has been started for you.

Day 1

Amy needs 10 beads to make a necklace. She has only 4 beads. How many more beads does she need?

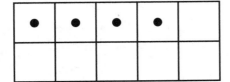

Amy needs _____ more beads.

Day 2

Jack needs 10 players to make a team. He has only 5 players. How many more players does he need?

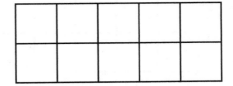

Jack needs _____ more players.

Day 3

Ellen needs 10 bows to make a wreath. She has only 7 bows. How many more bows does she need?

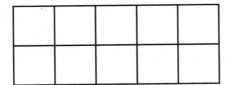

Ellen needs _____ more bows.

Day 4

The school needs 10 school buses to pick up the students. Only 8 buses are at the school. How many more buses does the school need?

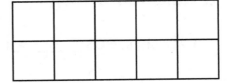

The school needs _____ more buses.

Draw dots in the frame to make 10 and help you solve the problem.

Olivia needs 10 buttons to sew on her sweater. She has only 6 buttons. How many more buttons does she need?

Show Your Work

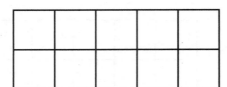

Explain Your Work

Restate Your Answer

Olivia needs _____ more buttons.

CD-105008 • © Carson-Dellosa

Strategy: Think addition to make 10.

Read the problem or have someone read it to you. Complete the number sentence to help you solve the problem. Day 1 has been started for you.

Day 1	Day 2

Day 1

Clara needs to make 10 loaves of bread for the picnic. She makes 3 loaves of bread. How many more loaves of bread does Clara need to make?

10 = 3 + ___7___

Clara needs _____ more loaves.

Day 2

Mrs. Cone needs to make 10 dresses for the play. She makes 5 dresses. How many more dresses does Mrs. Cone need to make for the play?

10 = 5 + _____

Mrs. Cone needs _____ more dresses.

Day 3

Quan needs 10 canned goods to bring to the food drive. He has only 9 canned goods. How many more canned goods does he need?

10 = 9 + _____

Quan needs _____ more canned good.

Day 4

Jan needs 10 forks to set the table. She has 2 forks. How many more forks does Jan need to set the table?

10 = 2 + _____

Jan needs _____ more forks.

Complete the number sentence to help you solve the problem.

Mom needs 10 lollipops to hand out to the children at the party. She has 6 lollipops. How many more lollipops does she need?

Show Your Work	**Explain Your Work**

Restate Your Answer

10 = _____ + _____

Mom needs _____ more lollipops.

CD-105008 • © Carson-Dellosa

Strategy: Cross out extra information.

Read the problem or have someone read it to you. Cross out any words that you do not need to solve the problem. Day 1 has been started for you.

Day 1

Katie blew up 4 balloons. Lisa blew up 3 balloons. ~~Dad put up 2 banners.~~ How many balloons did the girls blow up in all?

The girls blew up _____ balloons in all.

Day 2

There are 3 fish in the big tank. There are 2 fish in the small tank. There are 4 puppies in the crate. How many fish are there in all?

There are _____ fish in all.

Day 3

Brooke has 6 pencils. Her friend gives her 2 more pencils. Her mom gives her 1 eraser. How many pencils does Brooke have in all?

Brooke has _____ pencils in all.

Day 4

Uma finds 8 buttons. She finds 4 coins. Uma's mom gives her 2 more buttons. How many buttons does Uma have altogether?

Uma has _____ buttons altogether.

Cross out any words that you do not need to solve the problem.

Davis made 3 cards today. He made 6 cards yesterday. His dad made 4 cards. How many cards did Davis make in all?

Show Your Work   **Explain Your Work**

Restate Your Answer

Davis made _____ cards in all.

CD-105008 • © Carson-Dellosa

Strategy: Use doubles facts.

Read the problem or have someone read it to you. Use what you know about doubles facts to help you solve the problem.

Day 1

Melinda and Davis drew the same amount of pictures. Melinda drew 1 picture. How many pictures did Melinda and Davis draw altogether?

Melinda and Davis drew _____ pictures altogether.

Day 2

Mom made the same amount of corn muffins and banana muffins. She made 5 corn muffins. How many muffins did Mom make in all?

Mom made _____ muffins in all.

Day 3

Greg wrote the same amount of letters to his friends Amy and Ben. He wrote 2 letters to Amy. How many letters did Greg write in all?

Greg wrote _____ letters in all.

Day 4

A rabbit ate the same amount of carrots and peas from a garden. He ate 3 carrots. How many carrots and peas did the rabbit eat out of the garden in all?

The rabbit ate _____ carrots and peas in all.

Use doubles facts to help you solve the problem.

Cory has the same amount of pencils and pens in her desk. Cory has 4 pencils. How many pens and pencils does she have in all?

Show Your Work

Explain Your Work

Restate Your Answer

Cory has _____ pens and pencils in all.

CD-105008 • © Carson-Dellosa

Strategy: Underline the question.

Read the problem or have someone read it to you. Underline the question to help you solve the problem. Day 1 has been started for you.

Day 1	Day 2
Ethan played 3 games on Saturday. He played 3 games on Sunday. <u>How many total games did Ethan play</u>?	Oliver saw 4 kites in the sky. He saw 4 more kites fly up in the sky. How many kites did Oliver see in all?
Ethan played _____ total games.	Oliver saw _____ kites in all.
Day 3	Day 4
Wendy lost 3 teeth. Brett lost 6 teeth. How many teeth have they lost altogether?	Cole drew 7 pictures for his teacher. He drew 3 pictures for his friend. How many pictures did Cole draw in all?
They lost _____ teeth altogether.	Cole drew _____ pictures in all.

Underline the question to help you solve the problem.

Yuri counted 6 coins in his pocket. He counted 4 coins in his other pocket. How many coins did Yuri count in all?

Show Your Work	**Explain Your Work**

Restate Your Answer

Yuri counted _____ coins in all.

CD-105008 • © Carson-Dellosa

Strategy: Circle the numbers.

Read the problem or have someone read it to you. Circle the numbers you will use to help you solve the problem. Day 1 has been started for you.

Day 1	Day 2
Jill has ④ dolls. She gives ① doll to her sister. How many dolls does Jill have left?	Paul has 5 markers. He loses 2 markers. How many markers does Paul have left?
Jill has _____ dolls left.	Paul has _____ markers left.

Day 3	Day 4
Logan has 5 pancakes. He eats 3 pancakes. How many pancakes does he have left?	Kit has 4 candles on her cake. She blows out 3 candles. How many candles does she have left to blow out?
Logan has _____ pancakes left.	Kit has _____ candles left to blow out.

Circle the numbers to help you solve the problem.

Henry has 4 model airplanes. He breaks 1 airplane. How many airplanes does he have left?

Show Your Work

Explain Your Work

Restate Your Answer

Henry has _____ airplanes left.

Strategy: Underline the question.

Read the problem or have someone read it to you. Underline the question to help you solve the problem. Day 1 has been started for you.

Day 1	Day 2
Casey has 8 grapes. He eats 2 grapes. <u>How many grapes does Casey have left</u>?	Brady drew 6 pictures. He gave 2 pictures to his grandpa. How many pictures did he have left?
Casey has _____ grapes left.	Brady had _____ pictures left.

Day 3	Day 4
Mrs. Gomez has 8 pears. She puts 3 pears in her kids' lunches. How many pears does she have left?	Keith blew up 10 balloons for the party. Then, 2 balloons popped. How many balloons does Keith have left?
Mrs. Gomez has _____ pears left.	Keith has _____ balloons left.

Underline the question to help you solve the problem.

Allison has 9 toys. She leaves 4 toys at her grandma's house. How many toys does Allison have left?

Show Your Work	Explain Your Work

Restate Your Answer

Allison has _____ toys left.

Strategy: Draw a picture.

Read the problem or have someone read it to you. Draw a picture to help you solve the problem. Day 1 has been started for you.

Day 1	**Day 2**
The baby has 3 bottles. He loses 1 bottle. How many bottles does the baby have left?	There were 4 ice-cream treats in the box. Then, 1 melted. How many ice-cream treats were left?

The baby has _____ bottles left.	There were _____ ice-cream treats left.
Day 3	**Day 4**
Peter stacked 5 cans in a tower. Then, 3 cans fell off. How many cans were left in the tower?	There are 4 bikes for sale at the store. The store sells 3 bikes. How many bikes are left?
There were _____ cans left in the tower.	There is _____ bike left.

Draw a picture to help you solve the problem.

Reid has 5 peas on his plate. He eats 1 pea. How many peas does he have left to eat?

Show Your Work	Explain Your Work

Restate Your Answer

There are _____ peas left to eat.

CD-105008 • © Carson-Dellosa

Strategy: Use a five frame.

Read the problem or have someone read it to you. Draw dots in the frame to help you solve the problem. Day 1 has been started for you.

Day 1

Riley found 5 rocks. He gave 2 rocks to his brother. How many rocks did he have left?

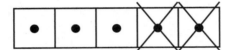

Riley had _____ rocks left.

Day 2

There were 4 people on the ride. Then, 2 people got off the ride. How many people were left on the ride?

There were _____ people left.

Day 3

Dad washed 4 cups. One cup broke. How many cups are left?

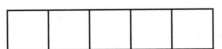

There were _____ cups left.

Day 4

Sally sewed 5 purses. She gave 1 purse to her friend. How many purses did Sally have left?

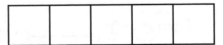

Sally had _____ purses left.

Draw dots in the frame to help you solve the problem.

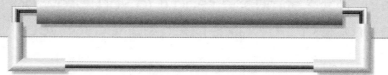

There are 5 children sitting on a bench. Then, 2 children get up. How many children are left on the bench?

Show Your Work

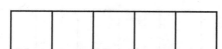

Explain Your Work

Restate Your Answer

There are _____ children left on the bench.

CD-105008 • © Carson-Dellosa

Strategy: Count back.

Read the problem or have someone read it to you. Count back on your fingers to help you solve the problem.

Day 1	**Day 2**

Day 1

Reece saw 5 crows sitting on a fence. Then, 2 crows flew away. How many crows are left on the fence?

There are _____ crows left on the fence.

Day 2

The mama duck had 5 eggs. Then, 4 eggs hatched. How many eggs still need to hatch?

There is _____ egg that still needs to hatch.

Day 3

Val baked 3 cakes. She gave 2 cakes to her grandma. How many cakes did Val have left?

Val had _____ cake left.

Day 4

Drew had 4 gems. He lost 1 gem. How many gems did he have left?

Drew had _____ gems left.

Count back on your fingers to help you solve the problem.

Joe had 4 pennies. He lost 3 pennies. How many pennies did Joe have left?

| **Show Your Work** | **Explain Your Work** |

Restate Your Answer

Joe had _____ penny left.

CD-105008 • © Carson-Dellosa

Strategy: Circle the numbers.

Read the problem or have someone read it to you. Circle the numbers you will use to help you solve the problem. Day 1 has been started for you.

Day 1	**Day 2**

Day 1

Lynn has ⑨ toy trucks. She loses ① toy truck. How many trucks does Lynn have left?

Lynn has _____ toy trucks left.

Day 2

Hayes has 8 action figures. He gives 3 action figures to his sister. How many action figures does Hayes have left?

Hayes has _____ action figures left.

Day 3

Malia made 7 bracelets. She gave her friend 4 bracelets. How many bracelets did Malia have left?

Malia had _____ bracelets left.

Day 4

Ty has 9 candies. He gives his dad 3 candies. How many candies does Ty have left?

Ty has _____ candies left.

Circle the numbers you will use to help you solve the problem.

Sara's baby sister has 8 diapers. Her mom uses 2 diapers on the baby. How many diapers are left?

Show Your Work	**Explain Your Work**

Restate Your Answer

There are _____ diapers left.

CD-105008 • © Carson-Dellosa

Strategy: Underline the question and box the key words.

Read the problem or have someone read it to you. Underline the question. Box the key words to help you solve the problem. Day 1 has been started for you.

Day 1	Day 2
Ms. Donna has 7 stickers. She [gives away] 5 stickers to her students. <u>How many stickers does Ms. Donna [have left]?</u>	Alex is catching bugs in a jar. He has 9 bugs. He opens the lid and 3 bugs fly away. How many bugs are left in the jar now?
Ms. Donna has _____ stickers left.	Alex has _____ bugs left in the jar now.
Day 3	**Day 4**
Davis bought 6 flowers for his mom on Thursday. He bought 3 more flowers to give to her on Friday. How many flowers did Davis buy his mom altogether?	Jane sees 8 bees flying aound a beehive. Then, she sees 2 more bees join them. How many bees are flying around the beehive now?
Davis bought his mom _____ flowers altogether.	There are _____ bees flying around the beehive now.

Underline the question. Box the key words to help you solve the problem.

Mr. Fin has 10 fish in his tank. He sells 4 fish. How many fish does Mr. Fin have left?

Show Your Work

Explain Your Work

Restate Your Answer

Mr. Fin has _____ fish left.

CD-105008 • © Carson-Dellosa

Strategy: Draw a picture.

Read the problem or have someone read it to you. Draw a picture to help you solve the problem. Day 1 has been started for you.

Day 1	Day 2

Day 1

The baby blew 6 bubbles. He popped 2 bubbles. How many bubbles were left?

There were _____ bubbles left.

Day 2

Roger had 8 gumballs in a jar. He chewed 2 gumballs. How many gumballs were left in the jar?

There were _____ gumballs in the jar.

Day 3

Mrs. Mabe had 10 tickets for the movie. She gave 3 tickets to her children. How many tickets did Mrs. Mabe have left?

Mrs. Mabe had _____ tickets left.

Day 4

There are 7 frogs for sale in the tank. A man buys 5 frogs. How many frogs are left in the tank?

There are _____ frogs left in the tank.

Draw a picture to help you solve the problem.

Erin has 8 books. She gives 3 books to her friend. How many books does Erin have left?

Show Your Work	**Explain Your Work**

Restate Your Answer

Erin has _____ books left.

CD-105008 • © Carson-Dellosa

Strategy: Use a ten frame.

Read the problem or have someone read it to you. Draw dots in the frame to help you solve the problem. Day 1 has been started for you.

Day 1	Day 2

Day 1

Ted has 10 cupcakes to sell at the bake sale. He sells 6 cupcakes. How many cupcakes does Ted have left?

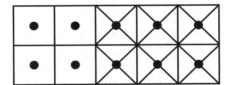

Ted has _____ cupcakes left.

Day 2

Ned gave his horse 7 carrots. The horse ate only 5 carrots. How many carrots were left?

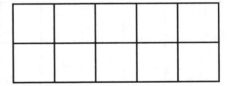

There were _____ carrots left.

Day 3

Eileen has 10 pairs of pants. She wears only 5 pairs of pants each week. How many pairs of pants does she not wear?

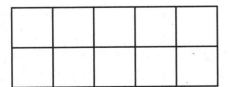

Eileen does not wear _____ pairs of pants.

Day 4

George has 6 shells. He gives 4 shells to his mother. How many shells does he have left?

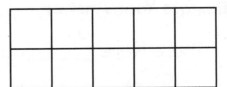

George has _____ shells left.

Draw dots in the frame to help you solve the problem.

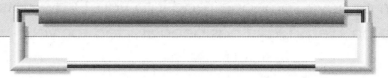

Julie fed her 7 cats. Only 4 cats ate the food. How many cats did not eat?

Show Your Work

Explain Your Work

Restate Your Answer

There were _____ cats that did not eat.

CD-105008 • © Carson-Dellosa

Strategy: Act it out.

Read the problem or have someone read it to you. Act out the problem with objects to help you solve the problem.

Day 1	Day 2
There are 8 dogs at the park. There are 4 dogs running around. The rest of the dogs are lying down. How many dogs are lying down?	Kristy saw 9 hippos in the water. Then, 3 hippos got out of the water. How many hippos were still in the water?
There are _____ dogs lying down.	There were _____ hippos still in the water.

Day 3	Day 4
Luke made 6 batches of slime. He gave away 4 batches of slime. How many batches of slime did Luke have left?	Victor saw 7 apes outside at the zoo. Then, 2 of the apes went inside their shelter. How many apes were left outside?
Luke had _____ batches of slime left.	There were _____ apes left outside.

Act out the problem with objects to help you solve the problem.

There were 10 snails on the plant. Then, 2 of the snails fell off. How many snails were left on the plant?

Show Your Work	Explain Your Work

Restate Your Answer

There were _____ snails left on the plant.

CD-105008 • © Carson-Dellosa

Strategy: Use a number line.

Read the problem or have someone read it to you. Use a number line to help you solve the problem. Day 1 has been started for you.

Day 1

The spider caught 10 bugs in its web. Then, 6 bugs got away. How many bugs did the spider have left to eat?

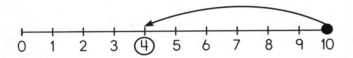

The spider had _____ bugs left to eat.

Day 2

There were 9 children at a party. Then, 2 children went home. How many children were left at the party?

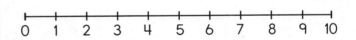

There were _____ children left at the party.

Day 3

Jen has 6 friends over to play. It gets late, so 3 friends go home. How many friends are still at Jen's house?

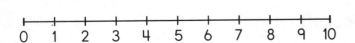

There are _____ friends still at Jen's house.

Day 4

Ryan puts 7 boats into the stream. He sees 6 boats float down the stream. How many boats do not float down the stream?

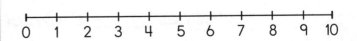

Only _____ boat does not float down the stream.

Use a number line to help you solve the problem.

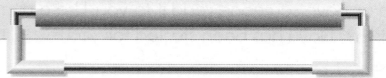

Krystal has 7 strawberries. She shares 3 strawberries with her sister. How many strawberries does Krystal have left?

Show Your Work | **Explain Your Work**

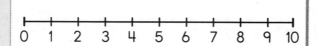

0 1 2 3 4 5 6 7 8 9 10

Restate Your Answer

Krystal has _____ strawberries left.

CD-105008 • © Carson-Dellosa

Strategy: Write a number sentence.

Read the problem or have someone read it to you. Write a number sentence to help you solve the problem. Day 1 has been started for you.

Day 1	Day 2
Faith drew 5 pictures. She drew 2 more pictures for her aunt. How many pictures did Faith draw in all? $5+2=$ Faith drew _____ pictures in all.	Elise has 3 pages to read for homework tonight. She has 6 pages to read tomorrow night. How many pages does Elise have to read in all? Elise has to read _____ pages in all.
Day 3	**Day 4**
Jamal bought 4 robots. His friend gave him 3 more robots. How many robots does Jamal have now? Jamal has _____ robots.	There are 2 ladybugs on a leaf. Then, 7 more ladybugs join them. How many ladybugs are on the leaf now? There are _____ ladybugs on the leaf.

Write a number sentence to help you solve the problem.

Ling's mom made 8 strawberry pies. Then, she made 2 apple pies. How many pies did Ling's mom make in all?

Show Your Work   **Explain Your Work**

Restate Your Answer

Ling's mom made _____ pies in all.

CD-105008 • © Carson-Dellosa

Strategy: Write a number sentence.

Read the problem or have someone read it to you. Write a number sentence to help you solve the problem. Day 1 has been started for you.

Day 1

Dad has to wash 8 windows. He washes 5 windows. How many windows does Dad have left to wash?

$$8-5=\underline{\hspace{1.5cm}}$$

Dad has _____ windows left to wash.

Day 2

There are 7 cubs in the den. Then, 3 cubs leave the den. How many cubs are left in the den?

There are _____ cubs left in the den.

Day 3

Yuan has 10 pages to read for homework tonight. He reads 6 pages. How many pages does Yuan have left to read?

Yuan has _____ pages left to read.

Day 4

Lyla has 9 oranges to peel. She peels 3 oranges. How many oranges does she have left to peel?

Lyla has _____ oranges left to peel.

Write a number sentence to help you solve the problem.

Tomas has 8 buckets of popcorn to sell. He sells 6 buckets. How many buckets of popcorn does he have left to sell?

Show Your Work	**Explain Your Work**

Restate Your Answer

Tomas has _____ buckets of popcorn left to sell.

CD-105008 • © Carson-Dellosa

Strategy: Box the key words and write a number sentence.

Read the problem or have someone read it to you. Draw a box around the key words that tell you to add or subtract. Write a number sentence. Solve.

Day 1	**Day 2**
Erin and Drew took the same amount of photos on their vacation. Erin took 4 pictures. How many pictures did Erin and Drew take altogether?	Mom made 6 apple pies. She gave away 4 pies. How many pies did Mom have left?
Erin and Drew took _____ photos altogether.	Mom had _____ pies left.
Day 3	**Day 4**
Craig and Dion went down the slide the same number of times. Craig went down 3 times. How many times did Craig and Dion go down the slide altogether?	Evan has 9 toy cars. He gives Jude 5 cars. How many cars does Evan have left?
The boys went down the slide _____ times altogether.	Evan has _____ cars left.

Box the key words and write a number sentence to help you solve.

Savanna has 7 markers. She gives Maggie 1 marker. How many markers does Savanna have left?

Show Your Work

Explain Your Work

Restate Your Answer

Savanna has _____ markers left.

CD-105008 • © Carson-Dellosa

Strategy: Solve and check.

Read the problem or have someone read it to you. Solve each problem.
Does your answer make sense? Check your work.

Day 1	Day 2

Day 1

Franny borrows 6 books from the library. She reads 2 books. How many books does she have left to read?

Franny has _____ books left to read.

Day 2

Rick makes 4 jars of jelly. Then, he makes 4 more jars of jelly. How many jars of jelly does Rick make in all?

Rick makes _____ jars of jelly in all.

Day 3

There are 7 kids in the pool. Then, 5 kids get out and dry off. How many kids are still in the pool?

There are _____ kids still in the pool.

Day 4

Kayla played 5 songs on her guitar yesterday. She played 2 songs today. How many songs did Kayla play in all?

Kayla played _____ songs in all.

Name _____

Solve the problem. Does your answer make sense? Check your work.

Fiona put 6 white daisies and 3 yellow daisies in a vase. How many total daisies did Fiona put in the vase?

Show Your Work

Explain Your Work

Restate Your Answer

Fiona put _____ daisies in the vase.

CD-105008 • © Carson-Dellosa

Strategy: Use the CUBES strategy,

Read the problem or have someone read it to you. **C**ircle the important numbers. **U**nderline the question. **B**ox the key words. **E**liminate the extra information. **S**olve and check.

Day 1	Day 2
Rashad polished 6 stones yesterday. He polished 2 stones today. His mom polished 3 stones. How many stones did Rashad polish altogether? Rashad polished _____ stones altogether.	Jeff made 8 pizzas for the food truck. He sold 4 pizzas. His dad sold 5 sodas. How many pizzas did Jeff have left to sell? Jeff had _____ pizzas left to sell.
Day 3	Day 4
Delia has 3 hats in her closet. She has 4 hats hanging on her door. She has a pair of mittens on the desk. How many hats does Delia have in all? Delia has _____ hats in all.	Felipe catches 10 leaves falling from a tree. He drops 4 leaves. Then, he sees 2 squirrels. How many leaves does Felipe have now? Felipe has _____ leaves now.

Use the CUBES strategy to help you solve the problem.

On field day, there are 10 stations to visit. There are 9 kids jumping rope. Then, 6 kids leave to play kickball. How many kids are still jumping rope?

Show Your Work	**Explain Your Work**

Restate Your Answer

There are _____ kids still jumping rope.

CD-105008 • © Carson-Dellosa

Strategy: Restate the problem.

Read the problem or have someone read it to you. Then, retell the story in your own words to help you solve the problem.

Day 1	Day 2

Day 1

There are 6 dancers on the stage. Then, 2 dancers leave for lunch. How many dancers are left on stage?

There are _____ dancers left on the stage.

Day 2

Forrest put 3 strawberries in his oatmeal. He puts 5 more blueberries in his oatmeal. How many berries does Forrest have in his oatmeal now?

Forrest has _____ berries in his oatmeal.

Day 3

There are 7 koalas asleep in the tree. Then, 4 koalas wake up. How many koalas are still asleep in the tree?

There are _____ koalas still asleep in the tree.

Day 4

Dani picks up 9 shells. She throws 3 shells into the ocean. How many shells does Dani have left?

Dani has _____ shells left.

Retell the story in your own words to help you solve the problem.

There are 10 people on a train. The train stops and 3 people get off. How many people are still on the train?

Show Your Work	**Explain Your Work**

Restate Your Answer

There are _____ people still on the train.

CD-105008 • © Carson-Dellosa

Name _____

 Strategy: Color the units.

Read the problem. Color the units to help you solve the problem.

Day 1

Daisy picks this carrot from her garden. How many units long is it?

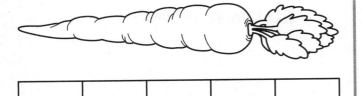

The carrot is _____ units long.

Day 2

Will pulls this crayon from his desk. How many units long is it?

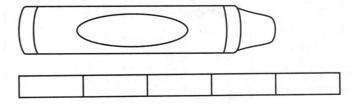

The crayon is _____ units long.

Day 3

Shawn wants to measure a coin he found on the ground. How many units long is the coin?

The coin is _____ unit long.

Day 4

Beth says the eraser is 3 units long. Chris says the eraser is 2 units long. Who is correct?

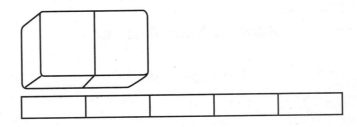

_____ is correct.

The eraser is _____ units long.

Color the units and draw a line to measure the object. Write the number.

Molly's dad asked her to measure his watch. How many units long was the watch?

Show Your Work

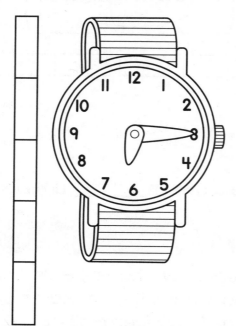

Explain Your Work

Restate Your Answer

The watch was _____ units long.

CD-105008 • © Carson-Dellosa

Strategy: Draw a picture.

Read the problem or have someone read it to you. Draw a picture to help you solve the problem.

Day 1	**Day 2**

Day 1

Hans told this riddle to a friend. This shape has 3 sides. Two sides are longer than the other side. What is the shape?

The shape is a _____.

Day 2

Mr. Walker drew one connected line with no corners or sides on the board. What shape did he draw?

The shape is a _____.

Day 3

Toby told his sister that he can draw a shape with four equal sides. What shape could Toby have drawn?

The shape could be a

_____.

Day 4

Amy drew a shape. Nell told Amy this shape is not a triangle because it is not pointing up. Is Nell correct? How do you know?

_____ because _____

_____.

Draw a picture to help you solve the problem.

Andy told Lisa that he could draw a square using two triangles. Lisa said that was not true. Who is correct?

Show Your Work

Explain Your Work

Restate Your Answer

_____ is correct.

CD-105008 • © Carson-Dellosa

Answer Key

Page 9
Day 1: 4; **Day 2:** 7; **Day 3:** 6; **Day 4:** 8

Page 10
Check students' work and reasoning.
9

Page 11
Day 1: 8; **Day 2:** 5; **Day 3:** 9; **Day 4:** 6

Page 12
Check students' work and reasoning.
7

Page 13
Day 1: 4; **Day 2:** 5; **Day 3:** 4; **Day 4:** 5

Page 14
Check students' work and reasoning.
5

Page 15
Day 1: 5; **Day 2:** 5; **Day 3:** 4; **Day 4:** 4

Page 16
Check students' work and reasoning.
5

Page 17
Day 1: 4; **Day 2:** 4; **Day 3:** 3; **Day 4:** 5

Page 18
Check students' work and reasoning.
5

Page 19
Day 1: 4; **Day 2:** 3; **Day 3:** 4; **Day 4:** 5

Page 20
Check students' work and reasoning.
5

Page 21
Day 1: 3; **Day 2:** 4; **Day 3:** 4; **Day 4:** 5

Page 22
Check students' work and reasoning.
5

Page 23
Day 1: 5; **Day 2:** 4; **Day 3:** 3; **Day 4:** 4

Page 24
Check students' work and reasoning.
4

Page 25
Days 1–4: Answers will vary.

Page 26
Check students' work and reasoning.
Answers will vary.

Answer Key

Page 27
Day 1: 7; **Day 2:** 9; **Day 3:** 8; **Day 4:** 8

Page 28
Check students' work and reasoning.
10

Page 29
Day 1: 7; **Day 2:** 6; **Day 3:** 9; **Day 4:** 8

Page 30
Check students' work and reasoning.
9

Page 31
Day 1: 8; **Day 2:** 7; **Day 3:** 10; **Day 4:** 9

Page 32
Check students' work and reasoning.
7

Page 33
Day 1: 8; **Day 2:** 7; **Day 3:** 7; **Day 4:** 9

Page 34
Check students' work and reasoning.
9

Page 35
Days 1–4: Answers will vary.

Page 36
Check students' work and reasoning.
Answers will vary.

Page 37
Day 1: 6; **Day 2:** 9; **Day 3:** 8; **Day 4:** 7

Page 38
Check students' work and reasoning.
6

Page 39
Day 1: 7; **Day 2:** 10; **Day 3:** 8; **Day 4:** 9

Page 40
Check students' work and reasoning.
8

Page 41
Day 1: 6; **Day 2:** 5; **Day 3:** 3; **Day 4:** 2

Page 42
Check students' work and reasoning.
4

Page 43
Day 1: 7; **Day 2:** 5; **Day 3:** 1; **Day 4:** 8

Page 44
Check students' work and reasoning.
4

CD-105008 • © Carson-Dellosa

Answer Key

Page 45
Day 1: 7; **Day 2:** 5; **Day 3:** 8; **Day 4:** 10

Page 46
Check students' work and reasoning.
9

Page 47
Day 1: 2; **Day 2:** 10; **Day 3:** 4; **Day 4:** 6

Page 48
Check students' work and reasoning.
8

Page 49
Day 1: 6; **Day 2:** 8; **Day 3:** 9; **Day 4:** 10

Page 50
Check students' work and reasoning.
10

Page 51
Day 1: 3; **Day 2:** 3; **Day 3:** 2; **Day 4:** 1

Page 52
Check students' work and reasoning.
3

Page 53
Day 1: 6; **Day 2:** 4; **Day 3:** 5; **Day 4:** 8

Page 54
Check students' work and reasoning.
5

Page 55
Day 1: 2; **Day 2:** 3; **Day 3:** 2; **Day 4:** 1

Page 56
Check students' work and reasoning.
4

Page 57
Day 1: 3; **Day 2:** 2; **Day 3:** 3; **Day 4:** 4

Page 58
Check students' work and reasoning.
3

Page 59
Day 1: 3; **Day 2:** 1; **Day 3:** 1; **Day 4:** 3

Page 60
Check students' work and reasoning.
1

Page 61
Day 1: 8; **Day 2:** 5; **Day 3:** 3; **Day 4:** 6

Page 62
Check students' work and reasoning.
6

Answer Key

Page 63
Day 1: 2; **Day 2:** 6; **Day 3:** 9; **Day 4:** 10

Page 64
Check students' work and reasoning.
6

Page 65
Day 1: 4; **Day 2:** 6; **Day 3:** 7; **Day 4:** 2

Page 66
Check students' work and reasoning.
5

Page 67
Day 1: 4; **Day 2:** 2; **Day 3:** 5; **Day 4:** 2

Page 68
Check students' work and reasoning.
3

Page 69
Day 1: 4; **Day 2:** 6; **Day 3:** 2; **Day 4:** 5

Page 70
Check students' work and reasoning.
8

Page 71
Day 1: 4; **Day 2:** 7; **Day 3:** 3; **Day 4:** 1

Page 72
Check students' work and reasoning.
4

Page 73
Check students' number sentences.
Day 1: 7; **Day 2:** 9; **Day 3:** 7; **Day 4:** 9

Page 74
Check students' work and reasoning.
10

Page 75
Check students' number sentences.
Day 1: 3; **Day 2:** 4; **Day 3:** 4; **Day 4:** 6

Page 76
Check students' work and reasoning.
2

Page 77
Day 1: 8; **Day 2:** 2; **Day 3:** 6; **Day 4:** 4

Page 78
Check students' work and reasoning.
6

Page 79
Day 1: 4; **Day 2:** 8; **Day 3:** 2; **Day 4:** 7

CD-105008 • © Carson-Dellosa

Answer Key

Page 80
Check students' work and reasoning.
9

Page 81
Day 1: 8; **Day 2:** 4; **Day 3:** 7; **Day 4:** 6

Page 82
Check students' work and reasoning.
3

Page 83
Day 1: 4; **Day 2:** 8; **Day 3:** 3; **Day 4:** 6

Page 84
Check students' work and reasoning.
7

Page 85
Day 1: 5; **Day 2:** 4; **Day 3:** 1;
Day 4: Chris, 2

Page 86
Check students' work and reasoning.
4

Page 87
Day 1: triangle; **Day 2:** circle or oval; **Day 3:** square, rectangle, trapezoid, or parallelogram; **Day 4:** Answers will vary but may include no, because a triangle is a three-sided figure no matter how it is turned.

Page 88
Check students' work and reasoning.
Andy

CD-105008 • © Carson-Dellosa

Notes

CD-105008 • © Carson-Dellosa

CD-105008 • © Carson-Dellosa